Anxious ANNiE

By **Cali Werner**
Illustrated by **Fer Peralta**

AuthorHouse™
1663 Liberty Drive
Bloomington, IN 47403
www.authorhouse.com
Phone: 833-262-8899

Because of the dynamic nature of the Internet, any web addresses or links contained in this book may have changed
since publication and may no longer be valid. The views expressed in this work are solely those of the author and do
not necessarily reflect the views of the publisher, and the publisher hereby disclaims any responsibility for them.

Any people depicted in stock imagery provided by Getty Images are models,
and such images are being used for illustrative purposes only.
Certain stock imagery © Getty Images.

This book is printed on acid-free paper.

ISBN: 978-1-6655-2377-6 (sc)
978-1-6655-2378-3 (e)

Print information available on the last page.

Published by AuthorHouse 04/27/2021

authorHOUSE®

This book is designated to
everyone that has always believed in me
even when I didn't believe in myself.

-Cali

Annie loves to run and is known for being fast.

She runs every race with all of her heart as if it were her last.

Racing was not always as easy for Annie as it is today.

Her fear and anxiety held her back,
making her dread race day.

Annie's anxiety began when she had to race against more kids than ever before.

She felt so afraid and said she did not want to run anymore.

Annie put so much pressure
on herself to be the very best.

Her fear was that if someone passed her, others might love her less.

Since Annie thought she was only
liked for her accomplishments,
her anxiety continued to worsen.

What Annie did not know
was that everyone loved her
for who she was as a person.

ANNIE ♥

♥ ANNIE
YOU ARE THE
BEST ♥

GO! ☺
♥ ANNIE

WE
LOVE YOU
ANNIE!

ANNIE

ANNIE
IS
THE
BEST

ANNIE ♥

RUN
ANNIE
RUN

Annie stopped doing what she loved
because she did not want to lose.

So, Coach Dana sat her down and gave her some very helpful news.

Coach Dana said, "You only lose in life when you stop doing what you love most."

"Whether you win or lose, the people that care about you will continue to stay close."

"Your loved ones are proud of you
for who you are, not for what you do."

"And if you do the best you can,
you should be proud of yourself, too."

Annie gathered all of her courage
and decided to lace up her shoes.

She told herself with a new mindset,
"If I give my best effort, I have nothing to lose."

Annie lined up at the starting line
with excitement instead of fear.

The announcer yelled, "Ready, set, go!" and Annie took off, listening to the crowd cheer.

The race was fun for Annie because she had a better mindset.

She knew that she would do her best, but that it was impossible to be perfect.

Every step that Annie took was a step for her to be proud of.

She smiled when she thought of her strength,
and her heart filled with self-love.

Annie crossed the finish line
with her fastest time yet.

She was excited that she did her best
and finished with no regret.

Annie continues to run the best she can, although she does not win every race.

With each experience, her confidence grows,
and to Annie, that is the real first place.

Printed in the United States
by Baker & Taylor Publisher Services